Thomas Jefferson

SADDLEBACK
EDUCATIONAL PUBLISHING

Saddleback's Graphic Biographies

ISBN-13: 978-1-59905-229-8
ISBN-10: 1-59905-229-6
eBook: 978-1-60291-592-3

Printed in Guangzhou, China
NOR/0614/CA21400935

18 17 16 15 14   4 5 6 7 8 9

In seventeen days, young Thomas Jefferson put on paper a one-page document that changed the world. It was the Declaration of Independence. It told why the American people would fight the British and King George for their freedom.

On July 4, 1776, the Liberty Bell rang out from Independence Hall in Philadelphia, where the Continental Congress was meeting.

Bong, Bong

Listen! They've passed the Declaration of Independence.

We'll fight for our freedom. It's official!

Post riders rode away, north and south, to carry copies to every American colony.

In every town the paper was read aloud.

We hold these truths to be self-evident, that all men are created equal ...

It has a fine sound. Who wrote it?

Thomas Jefferson, a red-headed 33-year-old Virginian, they say.

The first thing Tom Jefferson remembered was a day when his family moved from one plantation home to another one.

Here you go, Tom! This will be a long horseback rider for a two-year-old.

Before long, his father taught him to be a good rider.

Good work, son! Soon I'll enter you in a real fox hunt.

He taught Tom to befriend the Native Americans who sometimes camped nearby.

Chief, this is my son, Thomas.

How kolah.

Peter Jefferson was a surveyor as well as a farmer. Tom loved to hear about his trips into the wilderness.

Yes, there are mountains and cliffs and swamps and wild animals beyond counting!

I'd like to explore the whole country someday.

4

When Tom was fourteen, his father died suddenly. Tom was the man of the family. He was helped by his teacher, the Reverend James Maury.

I am afraid I don't know enough to run a big plantation.

You will find your father has taught you well. And his executors will help you.

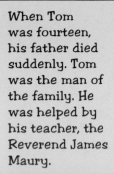

Under Tom's management the plantation continued to support the family comfortably.

When Tom was seventeen, they talked of his future.

Tom, I've taught you as much as I can. You have a fine mind. You should go to college.

I'd like that! And it's what my father wanted. But what about Shadwell?

Things are running smoothly. You have good overseers. Your mother feels she can manage.

Then I'll do it! I want to learn about everything.

There were three colleges in America. Tom went to the nearest one, William and Mary. It was several days ride from Shadwell.

I'll reach the Dandridge's home tonight. I'm sure they'll give me a bed.

William and Mary was in Williamsburg, the capital of Virginia and a town of two or three hundred houses.

Why, it's a big city!

Tom took an examination and entered college as a junior. He talked to other students.

I thought there were seven professors but I've seen only one.

Two of them were fired for fighting. Two or three others are in England suing the college trustees. And the president himself has become a drunkard.

It's lucky that the one I've seen, William Small, seems able to teach every subject.

Yes, the great Scot knows everything from mathematics and physics to grammar and astronomy!

And he seems to have a great mind as well as great knowledge.

And William Small was favorably impressed by his new student. He spoke of him to his close friends, George Wythe and Francis Fauquier, the royal governor of Virginia.

He has a fine mind. He will become a great man!

Very well, bring him to dine with us!

Tom became a friend of all three, sharing their dinners and their conversations.

And someday you must visit London and Paris, of course.

Later, Tom would say that at Fauquier's dinner table he heard more good sense, more rational and philosophical conversations than at any other time in his life. He learned facts and ideas, manners and morals.

Also he played the violin with an amateur music group.

He danced at many balls.

He went to many plays.

At the end of the year, he was not satisfied. He talked to his friend, Dabney Carr.

I wasted too much time and money. Next year, I'll study fifteen hours a day.

And that is what he did, getting up at dawn each morning.

Until eight o'clock I will study agriculture, chemistry, anatomy, zoology, botany, ethics, and religion.

From eight to twelve he read law; from twelve to one he read politics; and in the afternoon he studied history.

Come hunting with me, Tom!

Sorry, Dabney, my schedule won't allow it.

But every afternoon he ran to a marker a mile beyond the town limits and back again.

There he goes, regular as clockwork.

From dark until bedtime he spent his time reading poetry, drama, and literary criticism.
At the age of nineteen, he was one of the best educated men in Virginia.

After he graduated from college, he went home to Shadwell. He talked with Jane, his favorite sister.

What will you do next?

Become a lawyer, I suppose.

Will you go to law school?

There are none. One goes to work for a lawyer, reads his law books, helps with his cases until one day one knows enough about it to pass the bar examination!

It was arranged for Tom to read law in the office of George Wythe. He was one of the best-known lawyers in Virginia.

You will start with *Coke Upon Littleton*. You must read Coke and conquer Coke! Coke is the lawyer's primer.

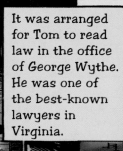

For five years, Tom studied hard. But he found time for fun, too. He danced, played his fiddle, fell in love.

Rebecca is so wonderful! Perhaps tonight at the dance I will propose marriage, and ask her to wait for me.

I don't think Rebecca wants to wait. She has just become engaged to marry Jacquelin Ambler.

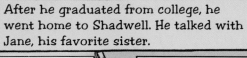

In 1767 at the age of twenty-four, Tom became a lawyer himself. He also began another project.

Here, on the highest point of my land, I plan to build the perfect house! I will call it Monticello.*

I will be architect, builder, landscape gardener, everything!

I wish you luck.

In 1770 a fire destroyed the house at Shadwell.

The news was brought to Tom in Williamsburg.

The family is safe?

Everybody is safe, sir. But everything burned up, all your books, everything but your fiddle!

I won't rebuild Shadwell. I'll put my time and money into building Monticello.

* *monticello* means "hillock" or "little mountain" in Italian

That year, Tom fell in love with a beautiful young widow, Martha Wayles Skelton.

Tom told her of his plans for Monticello.

Only a one room brick cottage is finished, but it will be a happy place.

On New Year's Day 1772 they were married at her home, the Forest. The wedding was a joyful festival.

Soon after, Tom and Martha left for Monticello, two hundred miles away. Virginia was covered with a record three-foot snowfall.

I think we'll have to ride horseback. Are you willing?

It will be an adventure!

All night the horses struggled through deep snow and up a mountain track.

We're almost there, I think. Can you make it?

I'm all right, my love.

Reaching the cottage, Tom quickly built a fire.

Look behind those books and you'll find a bottle of wine.

It was the beginning of ten years of great happiness.

To my dear wife!

To my husband and the years ahead.

Tom studied architecture, measured, drew plans.

The central house is here with 48-foot wings on each side but the service wings will be largely hidden, as Palladio* suggests.

* a famous Italian architect whose books Jefferson studied

Foundations were blasted and dug out of the clay soil.

Another twenty feet in this direction.

Yes, sir.

Nearly everything was made on the place, including the bricks.

Good! This is just the quality I want.

There were many social events.

Babies were born to them.

A daughter! We will name her Martha.

Altogether, six children were born; but three of them died in infancy.

Tom also had a busy law practice. And he was elected to the House of Burgesses, which met in Williamsburg and made many of Virginia's laws.

I haven't time for politics, but our quarrel with England has become so threatening, I must take my place in the House.

In Williamsburg he talked with his friends.

With his new laws and taxes, King George is treating us like slaves instead of free Englishmen.

What are the other colonies doing to oppose England?

We should form a correspondence committee to write the other colonies and keep informed of their actions.

I second the motion.

The Committees of Correspondence helped bring the colonies together in their fight against England.

In March 1775 Jefferson listened to a speech by Patrick Henry.

Give me liberty or give me death!

News of his words echoed through the colonies. They were followed by the shots of the Massachusetts farmers who fired on British troops. The colonies would fight! The American Revolution had begun.

The leaders from each colony met in Philadelphia as the Continental Congress. Jefferson was one of them. They chose George Washington to command the army.

In 1776 Congress met again. They chose a committee to write down what America was fighting for.

I nominate John Adams of Massachusetts.

Benjamin Franklin.

Thomas Jefferson of Virginia.

The committee asked Jefferson to do the writing. He worked for seventeen days.

His declaration was read to the Congress.

... That all men are created equal. That they are endowed with certain rights among these are life, liberty, and the pursuit of happiness ...

On July 4 it became official. The United States of America declared itself an independent country. People celebrated.

When his term as congressman expired in August, Tom went home refusing to serve again. His wife was not well. Also there was work to be done in Virginia.

We must change the laws: make them clear, make them good, make them fair—a foundation for building a true democracy.

It will take more than a Declaration, more than a war, to build a democracy. Our laws are still English laws limiting the freedom of the individual man.

What do you suggest?

For two years Jefferson worked on the legal code, helped by *George Wythe* and *George Mason*.

The law of entail allows a landowner to say that his property can never be divided even after hundreds of years.

By the law of primogeniture*, all family property is inherited by the eldest son.

These laws divide the country into large estates owned by a few men and worked by slave labor.

I want to see a country of small farms owned and worked by free self-reliant citizens!

Jefferson drew up bills to end entail and primogeniture, and they were passed by the Virginia House of Delegates.

* primogeniture is a system of inheritance by the first born son

16

Much of his work was done at Monticello, where a son was born in May 1777.

Sadly the boy lived only three weeks.

James Madison worked with him on a bill for religious freedom.

A man should answer only to God for his beliefs, not to any government!

Nor should he be required to support a state church.

A bill was passed in Virginia separating church and state and protecting religious freedom. It became a model for the country.

Jefferson drew up plans for: freeing the slaves in Virginia; for a system of free education; for doing away with the death penalty for most crimes. Some parts of these bills were adopted later.

In his spare time he did much building and planting.

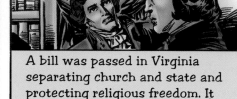

Mr. Mazzai has sent me an olive tree and four sour orange trees! We must take good care of them.

In 1779 while the war went on, Jefferson was elected governor of Virginia. The state had no money and no defenses.

British troops are headed for us here at the capital.

We must move the public supplies and records!

He worked with other men till early morning. Then he moved his family away. After riding for thirty-six hours, he returned to a spot across the river from the capital.

The British have occupied Richmond and are burning it.

But the British withdrew and the next morning Jefferson was back at his desk.

Richmond is not safe. If the British armies joined together, they could capture the entire government of Virginia. We'll move to Charlottesville.

The British general, Cornwallis had the same idea.

Colonel Tarleton and his cavalry must ride to Charlottesville swiftly and secretly.

They can capture the legislature there and Governor Jefferson at nearby Monticello.

An American Captain John Jouett, was spending the night at the Cuckoo Tavern.

British dragoon galloping west.

He rushed for his horse.

Only Charlottesville's is in that direction! I must try to warn Jefferson and the legislature.

I have the fastest, toughest horse in Virginia! I must reach Jefferson before the British do!

At 4:30 a.m., awakened by hoof beats, Jefferson came out on the east portico.

Jack Jouett! What brings you here?

For five hours Jouett rode over secret mountain paths.

He was scarred for the rest of his life by the branches and vines that lashed his face.

The British are just behind me. You must escape, sir!

He refreshed Jouett with a glass of water, then sent him on to Charlottesville to warn the legislators there.

After a peaceful breakfast he sent his family away. You'll be safe with our friends, and I'll soon join you.

Goodbye, papa!

Calmly he sorted and burned some of his papers.

He mounted his horse and rode away from the back door only a few minutes before the British galloped up to the front.

Jefferson's term as governor ended. The Americans won a great victory over Cornwallis' army and the Revolution was won. At last Jefferson could retire to Monticello and the life he wanted.

In 1782 he was visited by the Marquis de Chastellux.

Beautiful! You are the first American who has consulted the fine arts to know how to shelter yourself from the weather.

The Marquis wrote about Jefferson.

He is at once a musician, skilled in drawing, a geometrician, an astronomer, a natural philosopher ... with an amiable wife.

But all summer Jefferson's beautiful Martha was ill.

On September 6 she died. For three weeks Jefferson paced the floor of his room in grief.

When he came out at last, it was only to ride alone through the mountains.

His friends felt it would help if he were to get back into politics. He was named a representative to Congress from Virginia.

Tom, you are badly needed there.

The country needs good laws like those you drew up for Virginia.

He finally agreed to serve, and went to Annapolis where Congress was meeting.

In six months he did more to shape the United States than most congressmen can do in a lifetime. He proposed our present simple money system.

Everyone has problems learning to figure in farthings, pence, shillings. A system of tens, with dollars, dimes, and pennies will be easy.

He persuaded the states to give up their claims to western lands.

Virginia gives up her claims to all lands beyond the Ohio River.

He headed a committee to write a public land policy.

It is important that new states be formed and admitted to the union on an equal basis with the original states.

The Northwest Ordinance of 1787 including a ban on slavery after 1800 was based on Jefferson's ideas.

In May 1784 Congress appointed Jefferson a minister to France. He and his oldest daughter, Martha, sailed for Paris on July 5.

It's a beautiful new ship, the sunshine is wonderful, and the sea is as calm as a river.

In Paris, Jefferson loved the art, the architecture, the music, the culture, and above all, the books.

Look at this! I must have this one!

You've sent several hundred home already!

But he was shocked by the government and the condition of the common people.

Of twenty million of people, there are nineteen million more wretched than the most wretched individual in the whole United States.

We must have our own revolution.

Jefferson was still in France when the French Revolution broke out.

He traveled though Europe, taking notes on the latest scientific and mechanical marvels, the architecture, the animals, and the crops.

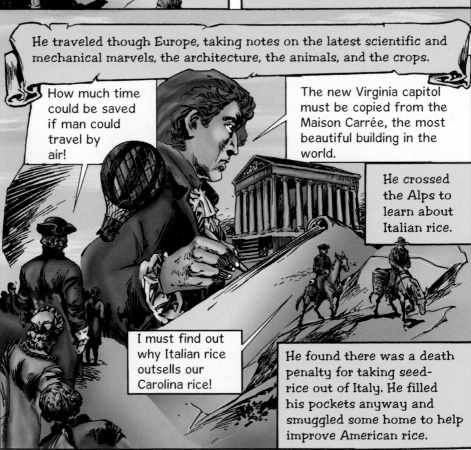

How much time could be saved if man could travel by air!

The new Virginia capitol must be copied from the Maison Carrée, the most beautiful building in the world.

He crossed the Alps to learn about Italian rice.

I must find out why Italian rice outsells our Carolina rice!

He found there was a death penalty for taking seed-rice out of Italy. He filled his pockets anyway and smuggled some home to help improve American rice.

It was December 1789 before Jefferson and Martha went home to Monticello. His people were so happy to see him. They pushed his carriage up the mountain road by hand, and laughing and crying carried him into the house.

No, no, my dear people you must not! Put me down.

In February 1790 Martha married young Thomas Randolph.

I am pleased! He is a gentleman of genius, science, and honorable mind.

A week later, Jefferson traveled north again to become secretary of state in President Washington's new government.

The Department of State will consist of three copyists paid $500 a year and two at $800.

Washington's treasury secretary was Alexander Hamilton. He and Jefferson had opposite ideas on governing. These viewpoints gradually became the programs of our two major political parties.

In 1797 John Adams was elected president and Jefferson, vice president. He was unhappy.

Adams is encouraged by Hamilton to take wrong actions and prevented by Hamilton from doing the right thing.

The time will come when you can change things.

In the campaign of 1800 Jefferson defeated Adams for the presidency. He was inaugurated on March 4, 1801.

In two terms as president, Jefferson changed the country in many ways. The most visible was the purchase of the Louisiana Territory from France.

Without a shot fired or a life lost, you have doubled the size of our country! It will open the west to settlers.

Now you, Meriwether Lewis, must lead a group out to explore our unknown lands.

In 1809 after forty years of public service, he went home for good. He rode, studied farming, and played with his grandchildren. He invented things. He built things. He entertained guests, sometimes seventy at a time.

The final 17 years of his life were devoted to fulfilling his favorite dream, building the University of Virginia. He was architect, surveyor, construction engineer, everything!

It must be the most beautiful university in the world.

He sent a scholar to Europe's finest universities to find professors.

Tell them at Oxford we must have only professors who are the best.

Nearly every day he rode his favorite old horse the four miles to the work site.

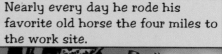

When he was not there, he watched the progress from Monticello through his telescope.

What do you see, Grandfather?

Bricklayers who don't know their jobs! I must teach them tomorrow.

The University of Virginia opened its doors to students on March 5, 1825.

On July 4, 1826, fifty years to the day after the Declaration of Independence, Thomas Jefferson died. He left a note of the words he wanted on his tombstone—the things for which he wished most to be remembered.

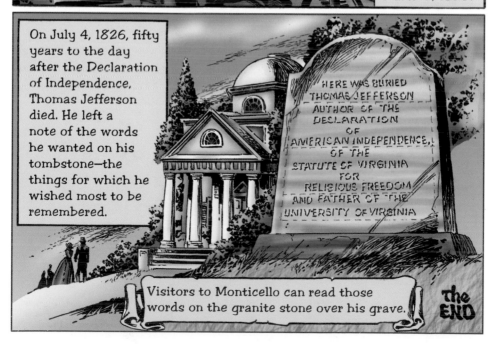

HERE WAS BURIED THOMAS JEFFERSON AUTHOR OF THE DECLARATION OF AMERICAN INDEPENDENCE, OF THE STATUTE OF VIRGINIA FOR RELIGIOUS FREEDOM AND FATHER OF THE UNIVERSITY OF VIRGINIA

Visitors to Monticello can read those words on the granite stone over his grave.

the END

Saddleback's Graphic Fiction & Nonfiction

If you enjoyed this Graphic Biography ... you will also enjoy our other graphic titles including:

Graphic Classics

- Around the World in Eighty Days
- The Best of Poe
- Black Beauty
- The Call of the Wild
- A Christmas Carol
- A Connecticut Yankee in King Arthur's Court
- Dr. Jekyll and Mr. Hyde
- Dracula
- Frankenstein
- The Great Adventures of Sherlock Holmes
- Gulliver's Travels
- Huckleberry Finn
- The Hunchback of Notre Dame
- The Invisible Man
- Jane Eyre
- Journey to the Center of the Earth
- Kidnapped
- The Last of the Mohicans
- The Man in the Iron Mask
- Moby Dick
- The Mutiny On Board H.M.S. Bounty
- The Mysterious Island
- The Prince and the Pauper
- The Red Badge of Courage
- The Scarlet Letter
- The Swiss Family Robinson
- A Tale of Two Cities
- The Three Musketeers
- The Time Machine
- Tom Sawyer
- Treasure Island
- 20,000 Leagues Under the Sea
- The War of the Worlds

Graphic Shakespeare

- As You Like It
- Hamlet
- Julius Caesar
- King Lear
- Macbeth
- The Merchant of Venice
- A Midsummer Night's Dream
- Othello
- Romeo and Juliet
- The Taming of the Shrew
- The Tempest
- Twelfth Night

SADDLEBACK
EDUCATIONAL PUBLISHING